Upon This Mountain

Prayer in the Carmelite Tradition

MARY McCORMACK OCD

With a Foreword by Eugene McCaffrey OCD

First published 2009 by:

TERESIAN PRESS
Carmelite Priory
Boars Hill
Oxford OX1 5HB
priory@carmelite.org.uk

ISBN 978-0-947916-09-1

Cover design by Bill Bolger

Typeset and printed by Joshua Horgan, Oxford

To my parents who taught me to pray

Contents

Foreword

Upon this Mountain is a profound book that goes straight to the essence of the spiritual life. To quote the author herself: 'If God is drawing me into intimate friendship with him, then he desires the ultimate meeting between the *real* person that I am and the *real* God that he is. All the vicissitudes of our prayer life are centred on the uncovering of one or other of these realities.'

This 'double vision', so to speak, provides the book with an admirable balance: between grace and nature, the divine and the human, God and us. Her message, we could say, is that in order to meet God – really to encounter him in a genuine and meaningful way – we need to be grounded in humble knowledge of ourselves and of our human condition. As she says: 'God...is not interested in befriending a persona, however devout or delightful!'

There is nothing negative about such self-knowledge: the more we are aware of our weaknesses, our vulnerabilities, the make-up of our psyche, then the at-first-painful truth will be truly liberating. The author emphasises: 'Human frailty of itself presents no obstacle to special friendship with Christ – a truth we strangely continue to resist, despite the combined authority of Matthew, Mark, Luke and John.' On the contrary, the more we accept ourselves as we are, the more we can meet God (and others) at a truly authentic level.

But this is not a book solely about self-knowledge, however vital that may be – and if we have any doubt on that point, we need only reread Teresa of Avila who asserts: 'I consider one day of humble self-knowledge a greater favour from the Lord...than many days of prayer.' But ultimately, this book *is* a call to prayer, to a deep and fulfilling relationship with Christ who dwells within us and who calls us to nothing less than life in union with him.

The author makes this highly perceptive comment: that union with God, which we think of as a goal to attain, is actually the starting point. She says: 'we often speak of "reaching" union, or "entering into" union. *In fact, the union was always there.*' But why do we find it so hard to reach this place? Because, as she points out, God dwells in our *depths*, and if we do not find him that is because *we* are not there. So she takes us into the mystery of prayer, to an intriguing, almost step-by-step experience of entering into stillness, based on her own years of struggle and perseverance as a contemplative nun. And she evokes the fruitfulness of prayer, both for our inner transformation and for the good of the world. She writes: 'It is not for herself alone that God's passion takes possession of [the person engaged in contemplative prayer]. She must mediate it to others, rather as the ledge beneath the waterfall takes the first impact of the torrent's force, which then cascades in foam over the rocks below.'

Mary McCormack is someone with very great experience of both human nature and the life of prayer. A Carmelite nun for over forty years, she has been President of the Association of British Carmels and has frequently held the position of prioress. She has also been deeply involved in the formation of younger sisters. To paraphrase the gospel, one could say of her: 'she knows what is in the human heart' (cf. Jn 2:25). She knows, too, a sense of awe at the mystery of God and she draws us to the One who matters above all: Jesus, who took on our human nature in order to share his life with us.

This is an important book. It is also beautifully written: clear, illuminating and lyrical, rich with the grace-filled insights that come from a lifetime of prayer – prayer understood as nothing less than a living relationship with God.

Eugene McCaffrey, OCD

Abbreviations

Works by Teresa of Avila

The Collected Works of St. Teresa of Avila, 3 vols., tr. Kieran Kavanaugh, OCD & Otilio Rodriguez, OCD, Washington, DC: ICS Publications, 1987, 1980 & 1985, including:

L	*The Book of Her Life*
WP	*The Way of Perfection*
IC	*The Interior Castle*
F	*The Book of Her Foundations*

Works by John of the Cross

The Collected Works of Saint John of the Cross, tr. Kieran Kavanaugh, OCD & Otilio Rodriguez, OCD, Washington, DC: ICS Publications, 1991, including:

A	*The Ascent of Mount Carmel*
DN	*The Dark Night*
SC	*The Spiritual Canticle*
LF	*The Living Flame of Love*
R	*Romances*
SLL	*The Sayings of Light and Love*

The Tradition of Prayer

The yearning of the human heart for encounter with God has led to an exploration of the mystery of prayer that has continued down the ages. Each generation of the family of believers, as part of its searching, revisits the wisdom and insight of those who have gone before. Each new generation also contributes its own experience of the journey to the source and centre of existence. We are never alone on this most solitary of paths. We are nudged along, taught and inspired by 'so many witnesses in a great cloud all around us' (Hb 12:1).

Carmel's witness

Among these witnesses the saints of Carmel are recognised as especially helpful and encouraging companions on the way. They have something to offer at every stage of the journey, supporting the hesitant beginner as well as the weary, weather-battered traveller who has been long on the road. Teresa of Avila and John of the Cross, drawing on the traditions that preceded and surrounded them but speaking out of hard-won experience, present a body of doctrine that addresses almost every aspect of the life of prayer. They speak with an authority that derives from life itself.

John was the son of a man who was prepared to sacrifice everything for love. Since Gonzalo de Yepes was not permitted to raise his bride to his own rank in society, he chose to embrace the poverty of his beloved Catalina, sharing her life as a weaver. Small wonder that John, the fruit of such a love, would later write in the *Romances*: 'In perfect love this law holds: that the lover become like the one he loves' (R 7). And he attributes to the Son of God words which might have been uttered by his own father: 'I will go seek my bride and take upon myself her weariness and labours in which she suffers so' (R 7). When John speaks of God's unqualified love for us, he knows only the language of tender passion.

Throughout Teresa's account of her life the presence and influence of friends is all-pervasive from her youth until her death. At certain times, her friendships were a source of danger and distraction to her. But without the inspiration and support of a great variety of friends she would never have embarked on the work of the Reform or been able to sustain the labours and difficulties involved. Teresa delighted in the love of friends and returned it warmly, but she also knew hurt and disappointment. Her many letters to friends reveal her fretting and worrying on their behalf, scolding and teasing, confiding and complaining. There can be no doubt that the friendship between Teresa and John, restrained though it may have been, was a stimulant to each of them on their journey to lonely spiritual heights. Teresa's own interior liberation came about when she finally stopped forcing herself to pray in the conventional way of structured meditation and allowed herself simply to enjoy a friendship with Christ Jesus.

Prayer and life

Teresa and John can teach with assurance because they have first of all learned the truth of who they are. Their words have the ring of authenticity, not least when they dare to articulate those experiences of the higher levels of prayer that are almost beyond the reach of words. It is part of the greatness of their contribution to spiritual teaching that, in their different ways, and for our sakes, they are willing to try to share what it means to live in conscious oneness with God. If they enlarge upon the experience of the degree of prayer that they call 'spiritual marriage', it is because it holds the justification for the demands of all their earlier teaching. They want to give us a glimpse of the life of the spirit at its richest and deepest so that we might be encouraged to embrace the cost.

Teresa insists that the prerequisites for a serious life of prayer are love of others, detachment on all levels, and humble self-knowledge. John is notoriously severe in detailing the purifications that must be voluntarily undertaken or passively undergone if we are to reach a true encounter with God in faith. They speak from an acute awareness that many people do not move on to the more mature stages of contemplative prayer because they are not sufficiently generous in responding to the divine work in their lives. As John says in his Prologue to *The Ascent of Mount Carmel*: 'it is sad to see them continue in their lowly method of communion with God because they do not want or know how to advance' (Prol. 3). But all are invited to go further, for God simply longs to pour himself into our emptied hearts and to catch us up into the radiant mystery of Trinitarian love.

Born to greatness

When we follow Teresa's description of the journey of prayer it would be difficult to count how often she says, 'His Majesty desires...' And when the bride in *The Spiritual Canticle* enters at last into the spiritual marriage, John opens his commentary with one of the most exultant passages in all his writings, entirely devoted to the joy of the divine Bridegroom. Using familiar gospel images, he demonstrates that this is the culmination of Christ's redeeming work: 'it is wonderful to see his pleasure in carrying the rescued, perfected soul on his shoulders, held there by his hands in this desired union' (SC 22:1). It calls for a divine celebration: 'Rejoice with me…!'

John expands in subsequent chapters on the sublime graces received by the person who has entered thus far into the mystery of God, and as he attempts to describe the indescribable, a sudden cry is wrung from him: 'O souls, created for these grandeurs and called to them! What are you doing? How are you spending your time?' (SC 39:7). So, we are *created* for grandeur. Every one of us is born to greatness, called into existence for nothing less than intimate participation in the life and love of God. It is a false sense of spiritual modesty that would suggest that we must not aspire to anything so elevated. And we cheat ourselves seriously if we settle instead for the small, tangible gratifications that can hold a more immediate allure.

In all the wide treasury of Carmelite teaching, it is these urgent words of John that constitute for me the wake-up call, the persistent nudge towards conversion. I draw attention to them at the opening of this introduction to prayer in the Carmelite tradition, in the hope that they may nourish in others a joyous belief in the dignity of our creaturehood and in the gracious invitation of our God.

Chapter One

Beginning to Pray

**Upon this mountain there dwells
only the honour and glory of God.**

In his drawing of Mount Carmel, depicting the
journey of the soul to God, John of the Cross
places this text at the summit of the life of prayer.[1]
Ultimately, all is gathered into such profound
simplicity. It is worth remembering, when one
seems to be confronted with a bewildering choice
of excellent methods of prayer, that all point in
the same direction and will finally lead to the
same goal.

Methods?

For many people, the rosary is their first practice
of regular prayer. The repetition of the familiar
words forms a background of vocal prayer, while
mind and heart dwell on the successive mysteries.
Some have other favourite prayers, which they will
recite slowly, making their own the sentiments
expressed. Scripture-based prayer, whether as
systematic meditation on a text, or in the form of

the now popularised monastic practice of *lectio divina*, helps one to engage with the word of God and so gradually to enter into 'the mind of Christ'. Another ancient prayer practice recovered in recent times is the use of the Jesus Prayer or a prayer word, either repeated continuously in combination with the breath, or simply used to recall the attention when it wanders. Any of these methods of prayer, faithfully persevered in, will gradually simplify and slowly deepen into inner stillness.

Those who turn to the Carmelite saints for guidance in prayer have often become confused by the multiplicity of books and methods and may be wondering if there is a Carmelite approach that would make the exercise easier and more fruitful. Or they may be troubled because prayer, formerly a source of peace and comfort, has become difficult and unrewarding, and they fear they have gone astray. It can come as a surprise that neither of the two recognised authorities on prayer, Teresa of Avila and John of the Cross, advocates a particular method. In all their writings, Teresa says very little, and John even less, about how to spend the time of prayer. Rather, they go to the heart of what prayer is all about: exposure to the reality of a self-surrendering God. They indicate some basic requirements in our way of living, if the encounter is to be authentic, and they chart the path of growing intimacy, leading to full union with God.

Regarding method, the Carmelite tradition allows great freedom, and the first thing we should learn from Teresa is to have confidence in following the way of prayer that suits us. She tells us in her *Life* how painfully she struggled with the structured form of meditation commonly practised in her time. It was clearly described in a work that was known to her, a treatise on *Prayer and Meditation*:

> The office of meditation is to consider studiously and attentively divine things, passing from one to another, that the heart may be moved to feeling and emotion for them. It is as though one should strike a flint, to draw a spark from it.[2]

Teresa observes rather wistfully: 'All who are able to walk along this path will have rest and security' (WP 19:1). She was not one of them. She repeatedly bewails the fact that she could not use her imagination to re-enact a gospel scene, or her intellect to hold an interior discourse about it, while the wandering of her thoughts 'tormented' her so much that it took all her considerable courage to persevere in prayer.

Teresian prayer

Slowly, Teresa learned to allow herself to pray in a way that was faithful to her innate gift for relationship, for being with another. Presence would engage her where reason and imagination would not. She describes to us in her *Life* how she prayed: 'I strove to represent Christ within me... I strove to be His companion... I remained with Him as long as my thoughts allowed me to' (L 9:4). She makes clear that it was not a question of picturing Christ, but of attending to his presence, in faith. She explains it as knowing him to be with her, as a blind person knows the presence of another in the room. She acknowledges that distractions can be a greater problem when the mind is not occupied in deliberate reflection, but she also maintains that from this formless type of prayer a person moves more easily into contemplation. To quieten her thoughts she found it helpful to read a little, or to have an image of Christ before her, or to look upon the beauties of nature.

By the time Teresa wrote *The Way of Perfection* she was convinced of the validity of this way of prayer and sufficiently aware of the benefits it had brought her to recommend it to her sisters in Carmel. It remains the simplest and most natural way of beginning to pray for any who have not already found a method that suits them. Here is the essence of her teaching as set out in chapter 26 of *The Way of Perfection*.

Mutual presence and gaze

Teresa writes: 'since you are alone, strive to find a companion. Well what better companion than the Master Himself...?... Represent the Lord Himself as close to you... you should remain with so good a friend as long as you can. If you grow accustomed to having Him present...you will find Him everywhere' (WP 26:1). We are simply to be with God, present to him, because this is what best allows God to be present to us as fully as he desires. Teresa was convinced that all her blessings came to her 'only because I desired and strove to have some place and time in order that He might be with me' (L 8:8).

'I'm not asking you now,' she says, 'that you think about Him or that you draw out a lot of concepts or make long and subtle reflections with your intellect. I'm not asking you to do anything more than look at Him' (WP 26:3). To look at him does not mean to form a mental picture, but to turn our attention in faith and love to the one whose attention never leaves us for a moment. It is a question of withdrawing our thoughts and desires from their absorption in other concerns in order to stay beneath the gaze of God.

Sharing with a friend

'If you are joyful... If you are experiencing trials or are sad...' (WP 26:4.5). Teresa would have us come before God just as we are. There is no correct pose, no required attitude in God's presence. Whatever is on our heart when we come to prayer can be allowed to be there, for it is already on the great heart of God and he lives its reality with us.

Teresa next encourages us: 'speak often with Him' (WP 26:9) and 'Consider the words that divine mouth speaks' (WP 26:10). We are to be very free in communicating with God in our own words, spontaneously sharing the sentiments that arise within us. But speaking must sometimes give way to listening and Teresa assures us that, when we have grown silent enough, the very first thing we will hear is that we are loved.

Being with, looking at, sharing, loving and being loved; these are the elements of Teresa's way of prayer. She describes it in typically rambling fashion, but sums it up neatly in her famous definition: 'mental prayer in my opinion is nothing else than an intimate sharing between friends; it means taking time frequently to be alone with Him who we know loves us' (L 8:5). The theologian, Hans Urs von Balthasar, makes this breath-catching observation: 'The wonder of this form of prayer is that it can and should offer the same personal contact with the Lord as men had during his life on earth'.[3]

Praying with scripture

Prayerful reading of scripture will always have a firm place in any serious spiritual life and it is the best possible preparation for the time of mental prayer. Teresa nourished her faith by reading, and it is certain that if she had had free access to the Bible it would have been her preferred book. A word from scripture can accompany us throughout the day, and there will be many occasions for pondering it in our heart, after the example of Mary of Nazareth. Praying the liturgy in the cycle of the Church's year will also ensure that the word of God grounds and accompanies our personal prayer.

In the time of silent prayer Teresa recommends that we represent Christ within us as portrayed in one of the gospel scenes, her own favourite being the lonely event of his agony in Gethsemane. She does not mean that we imagine the episode and go through it step by step, reflecting on its meaning and drawing from it lessons for living. She was quite unable to do this herself, though she considered it an excellent method of prayer for those who had an attraction towards it. What she advocates is simple attention to the immediate presence of our Lord, dwelling within us, here and now.

Distractions and dryness

In the simple, informal prayer of the heart's attention, 'the important thing is not to think much but to love much' (IC IV:1:7). Such simplicity, however, holds its own challenge. We can give very little account to ourselves at the end of our time of prayer and may wonder if we are doing anything worthwhile. It is true that the quality time we spend with a friend does not necessarily have any immediate, obvious result, but it gradually builds a friendship.

Teresa, having herself endured years of struggle, urges us to pursue the path of prayer with great determination, regardless of distractions or dryness, for otherwise she does not know how God can bring us to the blessings he desires for us. Dryness is that state in which our *feelings* in prayer seem literally to have 'dried up'. We are indifferent, bored, restless and would much rather be doing something else. Our efforts to stir some devotion are useless and may even provoke distaste for the whole exercise. It is important not to measure the value of our prayer by the delight and satisfaction it brings us. In fact, we cannot measure its value at all for it is unknown to us, but over time it will transform our lives if we remain committed.

Periods of dryness come and go. Distractions, alas, are always with us. Teresa frequently bewails her inability to keep her wandering thoughts in check. She likens this to having a madman in the house whom she could not control, not even for the short space of a Creed. She recognises that if our way of prayer does not engage the mind in any disciplined activity, we will be particularly at the mercy of distracting thoughts. What can we do?

It helps to begin well. Adopting a good posture is an aid to maintaining alertness, while attending to the rhythm of one's breathing has a calming effect. Some people find it helpful to have some visual focus such as an open Bible, an icon, a candle or a flower, to which to return when attention has strayed. Others will use a short prayer formula or word of scripture to recollect themselves. The important thing is not to try to fight distractions directly but, on becoming aware that the mind has wandered, to return our attention to the presence of God. We have to do this over and over and over again – 'just for a moment, if you can't do more', says Teresa encouragingly – until the practice has worn a groove in our consciousness and eventually the very awareness of a distracting thought becomes a prompt to recall ourselves gently to the presence of our Friend. The aim is not a rigid focussing of the mind upon God but a continual returning of the heart.

What of those distractions that are not a form of light entertainment but have a strong emotional content? Sometimes we come to prayer sad or angry, frustrated or worried. Perhaps it is some current event that burdens us, or it may be that in the silences of prayer some unresolved pain of the past has begun to surface. Our state of mind is not really to be regarded as a distraction at all, but rather as the very form of our prayer at that moment. We simply turn our eyes to God, allowing him to read the whole truth of what they hold, and by degrees we will be led to a depth within ourselves that is independent of the turbulence on the surface.

Prayer of recollection and of quiet

Both Teresa and John are very clear that our desire for God is first of all awakened by God's desire for us. If Teresa encourages us to turn our eyes to God in faith, it is because God is already looking at us, only waiting for our response in order to engage with us. John declares: 'if anyone is seeking God, the Beloved is seeking that person much more' (LF 3:28).

In the beginning, certainly, it can seem that establishing a relationship with God is all a matter of great effort on our part. We must set aside the time, go to our prayer-place, withdraw from all our usual concerns and focus our attention upon God. Teresa assures us that it becomes easier with practice, as the chattering mind and the roving imagination grow used to the summons to recollection and more readily obey, allowing us sometimes to remain quietly in the divine presence. If we persevere until the habit is formed, we make ourselves available to God's own action drawing us into the eternal stillness in which he desires to give himself to us.

It may happen during prayer, or even when we are engaged in our everyday activities, that a sudden hush falls upon us, an involuntary silencing of thought, as the mind's powers are caught and held in an inexplicable sense of presence. There is no inclination to do anything other than respond to this 'gentle drawing inward' (IC IV:3:3), as Teresa describes it. It does not last long and cannot be recaptured at will, but it is usually the prelude to a simplification of our prayer. It is the beginning, Teresa would say, of contemplation.

Prayer gradually becomes characterised by the ability to rest peacefully in a loving sense of God's presence, without desiring anything else. Words and ideas give way to silent communion. The flame of love is burning steadily and the most we need to do, if it seems to die down, is to blow gently. The heart's movement of praise or gratitude from time to time is enough. This new knowledge of God, freely given, is not even disturbed by the restless wandering of our thoughts, and it is best just to let them wander. Trying to rein them in will only result in losing the nameless peace in which one can still rest, at a level deeper than thought.

Jesus Christ forever remains our access to the Father, and Teresa insists that the starting point of all prayer is the humanity of Christ. It may be, however, that such a specific focus becomes reduced to 'a simple gaze at who He is' (IC VI:7:11), or as John of the Cross puts it, 'a loving attentiveness to God with no desire to feel or understand any particular thing concerning him' (SLL 88). This prayer of contemplative presence can become the norm for a person over a long period of time, and it seems there is no more to be desired.

Night

God however does desire more, and his further communication of himself can be a painfully confusing experience. All that we thought we knew of God seems lost to us, either intermittently or in a prolonged state of darkness and uncertainty. We cannot pray as before and we tend to feel guilty about it and to search for reasons why God has so abandoned us. John of the Cross is a sure guide in this 'night' and his fundamental principle is that, since nothing we can ever know, feel or experience of God is actually God himself, we are closer to the mystery of God when we can feel and understand nothing. It is as though God has removed from us the sunglasses that had reduced his radiance to a level with which our eyes could be comfortable. We are plunged into darkness, not because the light is not shining, but because its brilliance blinds us.

Having followed a way of prayer that consists more in loving than in thinking, we can find it very distressing when love itself seems to wither and die. But the same principle applies, and it is beautifully captured in the alternative Opening Prayer for Mass of the third Sunday of the year, which John himself could almost have written: 'Almighty Father, the love you offer always exceeds the furthest expression of our human longing, for you are greater than the human heart. Direct each thought, each effort of our life, so that the limits of our faults and weaknesses may not obscure the vision of your glory or keep us from the peace you have promised.' Knowledge of God, love of God – these are more than our understanding or feelings can encompass; and so, in direct encounter with God, thought and emotion have nothing to tell us. Only faith can accommodate such mystery.

John of the Cross likens this critical stage to the process by which a mother weans her child so that it may grow used to the solid food that will nourish its growth into full adulthood. Perseverance during earlier periods of dryness will have prepared us to wait in faith and patience as we slowly become accustomed to the less sweet but more substantial nourishment we are being offered. When we learn to stop struggling to recover what we feel we have lost, we will begin to be aware of the startling simplicity and immediacy of God's oneness with us.

Chapter Two
Prayer as Relationship

The most attractive aspect of Carmelite spirituality for people of today is probably the special emphasis on prayer experienced as intimate relationship with God. Teresa's definition of prayer as 'an intimate sharing between friends' (L 8:5) is well known, but others of the Carmelite family have their own way of expressing it. For John of the Cross, the entire spiritual journey is a deepening relationship between Lover and beloved. Thérèse relates to God as a trustful child to an indulgent father. Elizabeth of the Trinity's characteristic ascesis of interior silence grew out of her sense of intimacy with the 'Three' dwelling within her. Edith Stein is more reticent about her inner life, but it is clear that the courage and conviction with which she went to her death were rooted in her personal relationship with the crucified Christ.

Relationships human and divine

Relationships are the most significant factor in anyone's life; they are crucial to our earliest development and to our capacity to mature in adulthood. Our deepest experiences of joy and sorrow derive from our interaction with people, and we can generally sustain any amount of other privation if we have secure, satisfying relationships. In our times, when so much questioning and crisis surround the area of human relationship, Carmelite spirituality, with its sure guidance along the way of intimate friendship with God, has something to offer. We are accustomed to using the analogy of human friendship to explain what is happening in the life of prayer. Perhaps, though, we are meant to learn instead, from the pattern of growing intimacy with God, what are the dynamics of human relationships – and how to survive them! We have a whole treasury of Carmelite teachings that chart the path of this divine/human relationship, from a person's first conscious response to God's initiative, all the way to a union of love so profound that the person is transformed into God. The entire spiritual adventure is nothing else than the development of this relationship.

Person or persona?

God made us in order to be in communion with us, and it is in baptism that he initiates mutual relationship. If God is drawing me into intimate friendship with him, then he desires the ultimate meeting between the *real* person that I am and the *real* God that he is. All the vicissitudes of our prayer life are centred on the uncovering of one or other of these realities. It is not enough for God to relate to us at the level of our unconscious masks and roles; neither will he allow us to be satisfied with knowing him through image and concept, however lofty and refined. He will lead us further and deeper until, humbly in touch with ourselves in the truth of our own being, we are able at last to bear encounter with him in the very truth of his Being.

Inevitably, in the early stages of a serious spiritual life, we adopt a certain pose before God. We present, quite unconsciously, what we believe is expected or acceptable, just as we do before other people. We also direct our prayer towards an idea of God formed out of our experience of life, modelled perhaps on a parent or other authority figure, or influenced by school or church teaching. Growing familiarity with the Christ of scripture, together with God's own communication of himself in prayer at the level we are able to receive it, will gradually inform and deepen our concept of who God is; but it still remains a concept, coloured by unconscious projections and expectations.

Then something very disturbing happens. God begins to demonstrate that he is not interested in befriending a persona, however devout or delightful! He wants to engage with the person we really are. As he takes deeper possession of our being, he reaches concealed places within us, bringing to conscious level the darkness, pain and insecurity we would prefer to keep hidden. We do not need to have been profoundly damaged by life to carry a fair amount of negativity towards ourselves or to operate from behind barriers – and those we erect to keep others at a safe distance separate us from God as well.

The 'respectable' log

All of us have a deep yearning to be known and loved as we truly are, but we also carry the conviction that *no one* can love what we truly are, and so we are torn between hiding and revealing ourselves. In the silences of prayer, however, it becomes more difficult to hide. All manner of buried and forgotten things will begin to surface, and we can find ourselves caught up in emotional storms that overwhelm us by their severity and astonish others by their seeming immaturity. John of the Cross has the perfect image for this: the log of wood on the fire. While it lay on the hearth it seemed a perfectly respectable log of wood, just the thing for building a good fire! Once it is laid on the flames, its whole appearance begins to look less promising: it grows dark, smoky, a bit smelly, hissing and spitting!

This is the confusing experience most people have, not far along their spiritual path: that they seem worse than they were before, worse than they ever knew themselves to be. As John explains, the fire is actually driving out all that is preventing it from taking possession of the log and changing it into fire. It is important to recognise that it is not, initially, weakness or imperfection itself that is being driven out, but the falseness that would disown the reality of these. Human frailty of itself presents no obstacle to special friendship with Christ – a truth we strangely continue to resist, despite the combined authority of Matthew, Mark, Luke and John.

Inward, deeper, darker

Alongside this disturbing growth in self-knowledge, we may find that we are unable to connect with God in the same way as before. He is no longer a consoling presence but distant and unresponsive. In actual fact, he is moving the relationship onto another level. In the first chapter of *The Spiritual Canticle*, answering our desperate questioning as to where God has gone, John tells us that God is hidden in a person's own depths. If we ask why it is, then, that we do not seem to meet this God within us, John answers that God is hidden in our very *depths* and the reason we do not encounter him is that *we* are not there. We tend to live and pray on a much more superficial level, because the journey inward exposes us to more of the shadows of fear and anxiety that are lurking there. But that is where God is waiting for us; that is where God loves us: right there, where we thought no one ever could.

This pattern of revision – of our own truth and of who and where God is for us – tends to be repeated at deeper and still deeper levels, as the relationship grows more real. Often it will be precipitated by circumstances that confuse and challenge our sense of identity or of God: experience of failure or loss, for example, or of illness or bereavement. The 'dark nights' are never a purely spiritual matter. Major life changes, such as entering religious life, getting married, becoming a parent, involve loss on many levels – probably more so than ever before in these days of growing individualism. Such moments as these will, therefore, often trigger a new crisis in self-understanding. I think we see this demonstrated in Elizabeth of the Trinity during her novitiate. In the confused and overwrought novice, her former guide, Fr Vallée, could hardly recognise the devout young woman he had known. After this period, a certain artificiality begins to disappear from her letters; she comes across as a more robust person, more certain of her way.

Encountering the buried self

John mentions, just at the end of his treatment of the night of sense, some of the 'spirits' that can attack people at this stage: fornication, blasphemy, and confusion (cf. 1DN 14). With our modern understanding of psychology, we are less inclined to attribute these trials to evil spirits. They are our own demons rising up, the unacceptable parts of ourselves that have been carefully hidden away. *Fornication*: the wearing effects of prolonged loneliness and emotional hunger, as well as the actual experience of falling in love, can whip up a mighty storm of sexual need that seems to drown out the spiritual life. *Blasphemy*: buried anger can emerge as rage against a God who no longer fits our picture, as when Thérèse, describing her trial of faith, was afraid she 'might blaspheme'. She ascribed the doubts tormenting her to 'the darkness, borrowing the voice of sinners';[4] while she may have been merely listening to the voice of Thérèse. The sceptic sleeping in her may well have been awakened by the shock of finding herself to be terminally ill at twenty-four, or she may have felt impelled to question the certainties of her faith which had informed all of her life up to that point. *Confusion*: John is talking about an anxiety state, though perhaps our anxieties take a different form today: rather than attacks of scruples, the modern 'angst' and its moments of crisis tend to be around questions of faith, vocation and the meaning of life itself. The similarity with John's version is that the questions cannot be answered or quietened.

We do not negotiate these onslaughts without getting in touch with some very basic truths about ourselves – particularly about ourselves as religious persons – and without shedding a number of illusions. Teresa frequently speaks of the need for self-knowledge, and she always links it with humility. In fact, humility *is* self-knowledge. The word is derived from the Latin 'humus', meaning 'earth'. To be humble is to be rooted in the earth of our being, to be grounded in the reality of who we are. As Teresa says: 'to be humble is to walk in truth' (IC VI:10:7). She maintains that one moment of humble insight into ourselves is worth many hours of prayer (cf. F 5:16). For unless we know who we are, we will not be relating to God out of who we are, however many hours we spend in prayer.

The light of self-knowledge

The confrontation with our faults and weaknesses is painful as long as we resist the knowledge of ourselves that it brings. Once we can own and accept these less attractive aspects of our reality, we come to see that *they do not separate us from God in the least*. That is how he already knows us, and only our refusal to know ourselves in the same clear light impedes the growth of our friendship with him. When we can see our poverty and fallibility shot through with God's love, and can integrate them into our prayer, then we are finally reconciled with ourselves and become more authentic people. As a result, our relationships with other people become more transparent and genuine and we are better able to let them, too, be who they truly are. In this is the slow working out of our personal redemption in Christ.

The process that seeks to free us from false images of ourselves and from our limited ideas of God has periods of particular intensity. One of these crucial points tends to come as an aspect of the night of spirit. It is one thing to come to terms with our defectiveness – our dark, unlovely self – and to open wounded places to God for healing. It is something else to be brought to recognise the hollowness of all that we thought was good: that for which we are appreciated by others; those gifts and qualities that have enabled us to make a contribution; the work into which we have put effort and sacrifice. When the action of God, usually again through life's circumstances, exposes the self-protecting, self-serving motivation that has always lurked behind the best that we have done, then this is stripping indeed. This is the deepest challenge to our sense of identity and it can seem like annihilation. This is the 'nada, nada, nada' applied to ourselves.[5] We may resist, we may try to salvage something from the wreckage; but ultimately we are helpless before this dismantling of our ego. Once this searing light has penetrated the furthest places within us, it can never again be as if we had not seen. We can only consent to live more and more in that light: to know that we are naked, and not hide.

The two are one

While the light is still blinding us along the darkest stretch of the way, it may be that God no longer answers to any of the names we give him, to our familiar way of relating to him: '…and even on the mountain nothing'. Here, we can easily interchange 'Where have you hidden?' (SC, stanza 1) and 'Why have you abandoned me?' (Mt 27:46). This is a real entering into the ultimate *kenosis* of Christ. It is a participation in his death, an anticipation of our own death, and a rupture with everything we have previously known. In this void of all that can be held onto – about God or about ourselves – God, who cannot be contained by our vision, is finally free to awaken us into his mystery, in which we discover our own mystery, and the two are one. What seemed like death is in fact the real beginning of life.

Where there is no longer any barrier between my essential self and the essence of God, there is union. Since we draw upon the image of human love, we often speak of 'reaching' union, or 'entering into' union. *In fact, the union was always there.* God created us as an expression of who he is. The falseness of sin obscures this truth; the rational mind complicates it; the very yearning of the heart creates the illusion of separateness. But in the stillness of utter simplicity we are one with God, because he has already chosen to be one with us.

Chapter Three

Into Stillness

I was once asked to share my thoughts on how I pray today. The short answer to that question had to be: it depends on what is happening today. Prayer and life are inseparable and only become more so as life advances and prayer deepens. Possibly, this is why those traditional 'methods of prayer' of earlier times generally began with an 'examination of conscience'. The phrase has unfortunate associations with guilt and anxious self-scrutiny. But since the writers were people experienced in prayer, they can hardly have been suggesting that we need to 'clean up our act' before making any approach to God. They were, of course, writing from within their own spiritual culture and using its vocabulary; but I think that behind the expression lies a sense that, in order to relate authentically with God, we need to be grounded in the truth of who we are.

Into stillness through awareness

Certainly, I find that the starting point for prayer has to be a brief moment of self-awareness: an acknowledgement of how I find myself right then – peaceful... troubled... restless... joyous... preoccupied... angry... questioning... Whatever the mood, this is what I bring to prayer, and unless it is fully owned and accepted at the outset, there will be a subtle undertow pulling at my attention for the next hour. I find it easier to reach this simple awareness in the early morning, when the oblivion of sleep has reduced the clutter of my mind and the new day lies all around like untrodden snow. In the evening, when events have created impressions and reactions of all kinds, there is a danger of setting off down any one of a dozen avenues: analysing a situation, sorting out a problem, conducting an intense, inner dialogue about whatever has surfaced. But this is still preferable to the vague distraction of unacknowledged issues that can persist throughout the time of prayer in spite of well-meaning efforts at recollection. The basic idea, however, is to acknowledge what is there and simply allow it to *be* there, not requiring that things should be different. The allowing is the first step towards stillness.

An elderly member of my community once told me that, on being asked by a retreat-giver how she prayed, she had explained, 'I begin by listening to the silence of the chapel.' It is another way of grounding oneself in the reality of the here and now. For me, it is the second step towards stillness. Having settled myself on my prayer stool or tree stump, and having taken on board whatever I carry within me, I stop to absorb for a moment the silence of the chapel or the vibrant tranquillity of the garden, against the distant hum of traffic or the roar of a plane overhead. Fully situated in time and space, I become aware of the rhythm of my own breathing. I breathe in the silence – and breathe into it – at one with the silence and with the created world around me. I often repeat slowly a word of scripture, either from the day's *lectio*, or simply, 'Abba, Father', not as a mantra but as a final gathering of myself into prayer.

Beyond concepts and images

John of the Cross has long been my guide in prayer. His 'loving attentiveness to God with no desire to feel or understand any particular thing concerning him' (SLL 88) is my usual contemplative practice. During long years of struggle and darkness, I finally learned to let go of everything else. In that time of frightening confusion, every idea of the God to whom I would direct my prayer just withered away, every interior reaching out to God in hope and desire was beaten back. I was reduced to such incapacity that, in the time of prayer, I could only *be*. In the end, there was not even the slightest flicker of anything that you or I would identify as prayer. Total darkness and a spiritual immobility that seemed like inner death pervaded everything. I even stopped protesting.

Very, very slowly (and words fail me here), I became aware that there was now absolutely nothing between my raw reality and the utter reality of God. I understood that any concept of God veiled him more than it conveyed him, and that my reaching out to God was only distracting me from the immediacy of his presence. It took time to adjust, and my initial experience of this new knowledge of God was one of great loneliness. It was difficult to get a perspective on a God so near. I wanted him to be just a little bit 'over there', so that I could reach out and touch the hem of his garment. My heart sometimes cried out in bewilderment: 'How can there be relationship if the union is so close?'

'Knowing even as we are known'

Liturgy, with its legitimate use of image and symbol, now became a need and delight in the face of the intangible and ungraspable in personal prayer. The word of God in scripture became progressively more alive for me as I submitted to the silence of God in prayer. Gradually, I came to recognise that moments of such formless prayer had a substance that deeply satisfied and sustained me. I also became aware of an effect in my response to life. That which Thomas Merton calls 'the deep and secret selfishness that is too close to us for us to identify',[6] having been brutally exposed in the years of helpless darkness, continued in a kindlier way to be probed and challenged.

Inner rules that had always governed me began to give way to something more free and authentic. As I learned to tolerate 'unknowing' in prayer, I became more at ease with the questions and perplexities of human existence in our uncertain age. I became conscious of a simple oneness with God that pervaded everything in life, without effort on my part, and there was also the beginning of a sense of oneness with the rest of humanity and with all of creation. John of the Cross describes the kind of quiet communion to which such prayer leads: 'Since God, then, as the giver communes with individuals through a simple, loving knowledge, they also, as the receivers, commune with God through a simple and loving knowledge or attention' (LF 3:34). Is this what St Paul means when he speaks of 'knowing even as we are known' (cf. 1Cor 13:12)?

Receiving 'nothing'

I have written in the past tense, even though I am speaking of an ongoing process, because it is easier to identify the broad movements in retrospect than to try to home in on the to-ing and fro-ing of life and growth in the present. One of the most useful things my novice mistress ever told me was that one does not usually remain for long at a time in any state of prayer. I find this reassuring in the face of the apparently will-o'-the-wisp quality of the prayer I have tried to describe. Precisely because of its simplicity it can sometimes seem elusive. There is literally 'nothing' to get hold of, and it is difficult to stay with that. I have learned, though, that only that which is sought after is elusive, and it is the very condition of this prayer that it can only be received. To seek it is immediately to define it to oneself, to give it a form, a name, a limit, and so to make of it something other than the boundless simplicity of God's gift. John of the Cross suggests that even the practice of 'loving attentiveness' should sometimes be laid aside – as if, slight though it is, it can yet be too strenuous an activity in the face of God's utter gratuitousness (cf. LF 3:35).

The problem is that human nature (or mine, at any rate) finds it difficult to let go of all control and simply receive. The lively mind, the hungry heart tend to go on searching, regardless of the fact that the spirit has already arrived and is content. And so distractions abound and restlessness prevails, and often I have to return again to the starting point: awareness of what is going on in me – of place... of breath... of the word... The trouble, here, is that this process of quietening down is very similar to what happens when we are settling to sleep at night. Brother Ass is sometimes only too quick to intercept the signal, and the hour's prayer can become a head-nodding session! By the same token, however, I find that the time before falling asleep at night is often the most prayerful moment of the day. Likewise, I have noticed that even when stillness evades me during prayer, I can be drawn into it very easily in the midst of routine tasks.

Praying through distractions

Distractions in the time of prayer are one thing, but there is a distracted *state* in which I find it impossible even to take step one of the preliminaries to prayer. When emotions are strong, it is easier to remain immersed in one's feelings than to step back sufficiently to own and accept them. To allow them simply to *be* already requires a degree of detachment from them that I have not yet quite learned. It can equally well be a pleasant disturbance, a sense of excitement or anticipation, an absorbing project – like writing a chapter of this book! – that will keep me for days at a stretch somewhere on the fringes of prayer. Despite a fundamental desire, I seem not quite able or willing to make the commitment of attention that involves surrendering the current preoccupation entirely and entering the stillness that awaits me.

Then there is actual resistance. Sometimes I find that even when my mind is tranquil, it will wander aimlessly, vaguely avoiding that place of stillness that is life at its fullest when it is reached, but which always seems stark at the approach. This reluctance has little substance however and, once adverted to, is easily overcome. Of another order is the completely involuntary resistance that I have come to recognise as signifying God's direct action within me, stripping away yet another level of 'securities' and simplifying even further my communion with him. In a strange way, such resistance just has to be borne as the only honest response to something I do not understand, and do not yet know how to begin to want. It is no longer outright rebellion, if only because experience has taught me that such times of helplessness and dark anguish have always led to deeper truth. The sculptor needs the resistance of the stone in order to release the form he sees within it.

Over-activity, distraction, resistance – these ensure that the moments of knowing myself one being with the very being of God are never much prolonged. And yet, somewhere just beneath the surface of all apparent obstacles, this reality persists as the whole meaning and substance of life, however obscurely understood.

I am with the I AM

I am aware that to try and express something so simple and delicate is to encumber it with words. I have seemed to make concrete that which is only fitfully, fleetingly glimpsed and cannot be caught and held even for purposes of explanation. My only reason at all for deciding to write this chapter is that I believe that very many people undervalue their prayer, disparaging it at the very point where it no longer offers any obstacle to direct encounter with God. If all we can do at the time of prayer is just to *be* there, then we must be content to sit there and just *be*. In that place, at that moment, God shares with us the divine name, 'I AM'. We are at the interface of created and uncreated being. Here, the love of God can fill and flood our whole being, sweeping away in its path every mere idea or expectation of God with which we could still occupy ourselves. And then, the desire that motivated the entire life of Jesus on earth begins to find fulfilment in us: 'Father, I want those you have given me to be with me where I am' (Jn 17:24).

Chapter Four

The Apostolate of Contemplation

All prayer is apostolic. That is to say, every 'raising of the mind and heart to God' opens, from our end, the channel of communication between God and his creation, allowing the flood of divine life and love to inundate the world. This becomes increasingly true as prayer develops into contemplation, although it may not be immediately obvious.

An apostle?

We can readily grasp that a person participating in liturgical prayer is praying in the name of the whole Church and is therefore linked to other people even beyond the immediate assembly. We also understand that by engaging in intercessory prayer a person adopts a stance of mediation on behalf of others and we can view such prayer as a form of apostolate. But what of that most intimate and individual type of prayer – contemplation? How is the person in solitary communion with God an apostle?

An apostle is one sent to proclaim the good news of the kingdom of God. Can it be announced in silence? Yes, indeed. Preaching and teaching herald the kingdom, but it is only actually established in the heart of the individual in whom God has begun to reign, and it flourishes to the degree that his sovereignty is unimpeded. To allow God full freedom to enter our life and take possession of it is to be an authentic, if silent, apostle of the good news.

John of the Cross

John of the Cross is very fond of using the image of a window to illustrate his teaching about contemplation.[7] He compares the person following the path of prayer to a window through which the divine sun is shining. As the obstacles to the sunlight's passage are gradually removed, in the active and passive nights of purification, the window becomes ever more transparent, allowing the burning radiance of God to fill the whole house with light and warmth. The rays of God's love are always pouring down upon the house of humanity, but they can only penetrate the interior through open and receptive hearts.

Teresa of Avila

It was Teresa's own faith in this truth that led her to encourage her little group of contemplative women to place their lives entirely at the service of the Church. In the militant atmosphere of sixteenth-century Europe, when Christian leaders sought to meet the threat of the Reformation with the force of arms, Teresa likened her monastery to a fortified city in time of war. The beleaguered lord can fight from it, confident that the loyalty of its citizens means that it will never be conquered. In other words, she believed that her nuns in prayer could more effectively strengthen the Church in crisis than could the might of armies (cf. WP 3:1).

Still using the metaphor of warfare, Teresa goes so far as to say that the contemplative is the standard-bearer, riding at the head of the force, unarmed and vulnerable. The standard-bearer does not actively fight but rallies the troops around the banner of their Lord and 'if [one] lets go of the flag the battle will be lost' (WP 18:5). In this way, Teresa gives a highly visible profile to the person engaged in solitary prayer.

Thérèse of Lisieux

Thérèse uses another image, perhaps more attractive and more relevant to us, in her famous declaration: 'in the heart of the Church, my Mother, I shall be *Love*.'[8] Consumed by apostolic desires that seemed incapable of fulfilment, she had reflected that the vigour of a body depends on the hidden functioning of the heart. She understood then that her vocation as a contemplative was to keep the vital energy of love ceaselessly pulsing through the Body of Christ. (Today, conscious of the interconnectedness of all peoples, we would want to extend that analogy to encompass the whole body of humanity.)

Pope Paul VI had understood this when he wrote: 'If contemplative souls are lacking, if their life weakens or wearies, a lessening of the energies of the whole mystical body will automatically take place.' So had Pope John Paul II when, addressing contemplatives, he appealed: 'Be with me. Be close to me, you who are in the heart of the Church.'

Growing in apostolic concern

A transparent window transmitting the sun; the standard-bearer of an advancing army; the hidden heart pumping blood throughout the body – these are not images of an individualistic spirituality, peacefully absorbed in a private experience of God. Rather they suggest an acute consciousness, at times an anguished consciousness, of responsibility for others.

It is true that many people, embarking seriously on their own journey of prayer, will simply be pursuing a deeper spiritual life, seeking a closer relationship with God. Initially, the question of whether this will be of any benefit to others might not arise at all; Teresa herself was first of all motivated by an anxious desire to save her soul. But one does not travel far on the path of prayer without a growing awareness of solidarity with all God's people, and this carries an awesome sense of mission. As our union with God deepens, we know ourselves to be one with all that is God's. We are brought to identify more and more fully with the needs and sufferings, hopes and strivings of the Church and the whole world, as we enter further into the prayer and self-gift of Christ who 'loved the Church and sacrificed himself for her' (Eph 5:25).

We can follow this development very clearly in Teresa's life because she chronicles its successive stages for us. What first sparked her desire to live her Carmelite calling more earnestly was the understanding that was granted her of the terrible suffering of being eternally separated from God. From her own dread of this fate grew her desire to help others also to avoid it. 'It seems certain to me that in order to free one alone from such appalling torments I would suffer many deaths very willingly' (L 32:6). Her anxiety 'to know the manner and way in which I could do penance for so much evil and merit something in order to gain so much good' (L 32:8) led to her founding the small community of St Joseph's in Avila.

Teresa opens *The Way of Perfection* by explaining that while the foundation was still in preparation, the news of the advances of the Reformation in Europe widened the horizons of her concern. She understood the Church's broken communion as an attack on her beloved Christ himself and longed that 'since He has so many enemies and so few friends that these few friends be good ones' (WP 1:2). Her own personal interests have lost importance. She writes: 'What would it matter were I to remain in purgatory until judgment day if through my prayer I could save even one soul?' (WP 3:6).

A few years later, her apostolic zeal was further inflamed on learning of the multitudes in the new world that were entirely without knowledge of Christ. She describes herself as 'grief-stricken' and 'going about with such great affliction', while she cried out to the Lord and begged him to give her the means to be able to do something (F 1:7.8). She recognised the Lord's response in the authorisation given her to multiply her houses of prayer. Somehow she understood that the spread of her Order in Spain had implications for the evangelisation of countless souls in the Americas.

The apostolate of witness

The person responsive to God's action in the grace and the struggle of prayer will certainly experience this development. Concern for spiritual advancement will slowly give way to an awareness that one is not drawn into the close embrace of the divinity for oneself alone. An apostle is one sent with a message to others, and the first message entrusted to the person invited to a deepening relationship with God in prayer is that such intimacy is meant for all. Steadfast commitment to prayer testifies that God is the full and final answer to the longings of the human heart, and that *God himself longs for us* and offers to everyone the experience of loving encounter with him.

Teresa even wished her nuns actively to encourage those with whom they associated to take up and to persevere in the practice of prayer, so that they too might experience its blessings: 'if they are disposed and there is some friendship, try to remove any fear they may have of beginning to use so great a good… It would be no small favour from the Lord if you were to succeed in awakening some soul to this good' (WP 20:3.6).

John of the Cross reveals the extent of his own zeal when he closes his description of the highest level of prayer, the spiritual marriage, with this heartfelt prayer: 'May the most sweet

Jesus, Bridegroom of faithful souls, be pleased to bring all who invoke his name to this marriage' (SC 40:7).

'Union with the prayer of Christ'

The *Catechism of the Catholic Church* opens up further reflections on the apostolic nature of contemplative prayer:

> Contemplative prayer is a union with the prayer of Christ insofar as it makes us participate in his mystery. (#2718)

Central to the mystery of Christ is his abiding communion with the Father. This is what constantly drove and sustained his service of the Father's will, that all should come to eternal life through him. The contemplative is called to enter into the same deep, filial relationship that saw Christ stealing out of the house in the early morning in order to find time and space to be alone with his Father. Those moments of silent surrender led him, as they will lead us, to the cross: 'the pure spiritual cross and nakedness of Christ's poverty of spirit' (2A 7:5).

What does it mean to participate in the mystery of Christ, if not to enter right into his paschal experience of dying and rising to new life? John of the Cross leaves us in no doubt that this is where the journey of prayer is taking us. He reminds us that the two disciples who sought places at the side of Jesus were offered the chalice he was about to drink, and: 'This chalice means death to one's natural self' (2A 7:7). John continues: 'Because I have said that Christ is the way and that this way is a death to our natural selves in the sensory and spiritual parts of the soul, I would like to demonstrate how this death is patterned on Christ's, for he is our model and light' (2A 7:9).

The painful, liberating nights of sense and of spirit constitute a death 'patterned on Christ's', leading to a more abundant inflow of divine life, which consequently circulates more freely in our world. John does not hesitate to identify this difficult 'work' of the contemplative with Jesus' work of redemption – 'the most marvellous work of his whole life… the reconciliation and union of the human race with God' (2A 7:11).

'A communion of love'

The next paragraph of the *Catechism* states:

> Contemplative prayer is a communion of love bearing Life for the multitude, to the extent that it consents to abide in the night of faith. (#2719)

The person engaged in contemplative prayer is in simultaneous communion with God and with 'the multitude'. Within her heart two powerful forces unite, the consuming fire of God's love and the hunger of humanity to love and be loved. It is not for herself alone that God's passion takes possession of her. She must mediate it to others, rather as the ledge beneath the waterfall takes the first impact of the torrent's force, which then cascades in foam over the rocks below.

Blessed Elizabeth of the Trinity had a very simple way of exercising this mediation and she explains it in a letter to a friend. 'I raise my eyes and look at God, and then I lower them on you, exposing you to the rays of His Love.'[9] This young Carmelite, drawn to a life of silence and hiddenness, had a strong sense of apostolate. Her letters and retreat notes are full of it, as when she writes to a young priest: 'I want to be an apostle with you, from the depths of my dear solitude in Carmel, I want to work for the glory of God, and for that I must be wholly filled with Him; then I will be all-powerful...'[10] Again, to another priest friend, in Advent: 'Isn't fire love? And isn't our mission also to prepare the way of the Lord through our union with Him whom the Apostle calls a "consuming fire"? At His touch our soul will become like a flame of love spreading into all the members of the body of Christ, the Church...'[11]

'Bearing Life for the multitude'

Elizabeth is doubtless influenced here by the teaching of John of the Cross, who also equates fire and love. When he presents the prayer journey as a gradual intensification and purification of our poor human love, under the action of divine love, the source of our redemption, he thinks of a log of wood slowly being changed into fire. The flames kindle first the outer edges, then penetrate deeper, and finally reach the very heartwood, destroying all that opposes their progress. Finally the log is so consumed by the fire that it becomes fire itself, giving the same light and heat as the fire, without any distinction – 'a flame of love'. It is from this point that the fullness of the contemplative apostolate flows. John does not hesitate to claim: 'a little of this pure love is more precious to God and the soul and more beneficial to the Church, even though it seems one is doing nothing, than all these other works put together' (SC 29:2).

John himself was a busy man, who often had to be engaged in 'these other works'. His point is that 'good works can be performed only by the power of God', and until his power is free in us our activity will 'accomplish little, and sometimes nothing' (SC 29:3). In the final pages of *The Interior Castle*, Teresa reiterates her conviction that the whole purpose of prayer is that we may have strength to serve those around us, but that our actions are only worth the love in which they are grounded.

Thus, John says, the Bride of the *Canticle* can sing:

> Now I occupy my soul
> and all my energy in his service;
> I no longer tend the herd,
> nor have I any other work
> now that my every act is love. (SC, stanza 28)

Or, as Thérèse would simply put it: 'MY VOCATION IS LOVE!'[12] In her night of faith she was prepared to fulfil this vocation even at the table of sinners, praying in their name in order that, from the very ranks of the godless, love of God might arise.

Love's fruitfulness

The fruit of contemplative prayer is a heart that widens to a universal embrace. To be so intimately one with the very love of God is to communicate it to others, after the supreme example of Mary, the God-bearer, *Theotokos*. Placing herself at the service of the Father's saving will, Mary literally *bore* direct encounter with the Word of God, in a communion of love, before 'bearing Life for the multitude'.

God is Love and he created us that we might become Love. What gives mutual love its fruitfulness is not strength of sentiment but union of wills. Both Teresa and John define union with God as the point at which the will of God and the will of the person become one. 'The supernatural union exists when God's will and the soul's are in conformity' (2A 5:3). And Teresa assures us: 'This union with God's will is the union I have desired all my life; it is the union I ask the Lord for always and the one that is clearest and safest' (IC V:3:5). This perfect harmony of wills is the flowing together of the energies of love, the ultimate generative power. 'A branch cannot bear fruit all by itself... Whoever remains in me, with me in him, bears fruit in plenty... It is to the glory of my Father that you should bear much fruit' (Jn 15:4.5.8).

To be one with God's will is to be totally surrendered to divine desire. And God's desire is for 'everyone to be saved and come to full knowledge of the truth' (1Tm 2:4). In our silent depths, freed at last from personal agenda and alive with this longing, our lives will truly bear fruit, to the glory of the Father.

> *Upon this mountain there dwells*
> *only the honour and glory of God.*

Epilogue
Carmel as Garden-Land

⚜

From biblical times down to the medieval beginnings of the Carmelite Order, there is ample evidence that Mount Carmel was a place of beauty and fruitfulness. The name 'Carmel' means 'orchard' or 'garden-land', and garden imagery is frequently found in Carmelite writings. Teresa of Avila describes the different stages of growth in prayer in terms of four ways of watering a garden, and in *The Spiritual Canticle* of John of the Cross the marriage between God and the soul is consummated in a garden. Thérèse of Lisieux thinks of herself as a 'little flower' in God's garden. So it is not, perhaps, surprising that when I stop to ponder what Carmel, the land of prayer, means to me, my thoughts take a walk in the garden.

The garden in winter...

A garden is a place where living things grow, not in jungle-like profusion but in an ordered and cultivated way. And there is always life in a garden, even in the apparent deadness of winter. In the bleak days after Christmas, down in a far, damp corner of the garden of the monastery where I live, a piercingly sweet scent fills the air. A large patch of winter heliotrope flourishes here, encroaching on the muddy path that is seldom traversed. Each thick, fleshy stem bears a head of flowers that could not be called pretty, and their slight mauve and grey tones show to advantage only against last year's tangle of dead grasses, but I do not know any flower of high summer that has such a powerful scent.

Some distance away, on the other side of one of the several small hillocks in the garden, there is a clump of hazel trees. Here, too, I always pause for a while on a January walk. A chill wind rattles the bare twigs and, almost casually, the pollen drops from the swaying catkin onto the tiny red asterisk that is the waiting female flower. Long before the buds have begun to swell on the fruit trees, the mystery of new life has been initiated among these stark branches.

Moving towards the centre of the garden, my steps are halted in front of a rustic 'hermitage' between two towering lime trees. Here, in a vivid splash of colour, are clumps of winter aconites. They will even thrust through a covering of snow, as if nature, to cheer the cold winter's day, had thrown a little tea party, setting out her gold cups in green saucers on a clean white tablecloth. The sight is a bold affirmation that spring is surely coming and there will be drifts of daffodils one day.

These small wonders – of perfume, of fertility, of colour in mid-winter – are short-lived and easily missed, requiring a special pilgrimage each year, in Wellington boots, under a grey sky. But when I have stood before them in wintry periods of my own Carmelite life, they have never failed to lift my heart. I think that one of the great contributions of the Carmelite spiritual tradition is its offering of a context for all the lack and loss and letting go in our lives; all that is seemingly negative and even death-dealing in our quest for God. John of the Cross speaks of a journey by night, Thérèse of a *little* way, the great Teresa of a silkworm hidden in its cocoon. We have repeated assurance that when we feel quite lost and weak and utterly unlike all that we aspire to be, things are as they should be, all is integral to our growing into God, and there are flowers that will bloom only in our winter.

. . .and in spring

When the snowdrops and daffodils have followed the aconites and gone, and we are into late spring, the slope behind the lime trees is slowly covered with primroses. There is something about their utterly simple form and colouring that makes me think of Carmelite beginnings, when the call is fresh and ideals have yet to be tested. It is the time of hope, enthusiasm and promise, but it is also an uncertain step into the unknown and the early outcome can be disconcerting.

Many of us come to Carmel already well defended against life's hurts and presenting a fairly acceptable front. In the silence of the cloister, however, cries that have long been hushed are apt to make themselves heard again, and carefully constructed barriers are no proof against a God who has already embraced the real person within and seeks only to draw her to recognition and acceptance of this truth. The loss of familiar ways of coping with life and the surfacing of buried pain can create an overwhelmingly frightening and confusing experience. A text commonly displayed in therapy centres warns: 'The truth will set you free – but first, it will hurt like anything.' Some people have to continue this journey into truth in a less intense way on other roads of life. Some remain exposed to the burning gaze of God in a primary commitment to contemplative prayer as their way to spiritual maturity. But the garden-land of Carmel knows no frontiers and all its paths lead onwards into a growing freedom in God. I never see the primroses fade. The summer grass simply grows taller around them and they are hidden from view.

A time to die

Opposite the hill of primroses there once stood a great weeping willow. This was not the neatly domed suburban type but the riverside variety, with branches that leaped and cascaded in tumultuous abandon. It was an ancient tree with a hollow in the trunk where a mallard duck used to nest every year. (We never did discover how she transported her newly hatched balls of fluff to the ground, to take them on their first brisk perambulation of the garden in search of water.) One night, when the monastery was asleep, the huge tree fell to the ground. It made no sound that any of us heard and it did no damage as it fell, but it lay with its branches flung wide, like a Carmelite on her profession day, prostrate on the floor with her cloak spread about her. The gracefulness of its dying was reminiscent, too, of the way an old Carmelite meets death, without noise or drama. I have sat by the deathbeds of so many of our sisters and I have seldom witnessed either physical or emotional distress. These were women in whom the long slow purifications wrought by the Spirit were nearing completion. If the depth of their union with God was often hidden from us by the limitations or the idiosyncrasies of age, it shone out in the perfect naturalness with which they passed 'from this world to the Father' (Jn 13:1).

One example must suffice. An old Lancashire sister lay quite still, her eyes devoutly closed, while the community around her said the prayers for the dying. After they had left the room except for a sister who remained at her bedside, she opened one eye and, with a quizzical look at her companion, asked, 'What do I look like when I'm dying?' 'Very pretty,' was the reply. 'Oh, don't make me vain at this point,' chuckled the dying nun; 'I'll lose a mark!' When she died, in the early hours of the following morning, as with so many others there was nothing to mark the moment of final surrender except the stillness that followed her last breath.

When the old willow died, the tree surgeons came and sawed up the branches. They piled the logs on top of the splintered stump and made a huge fire. All that remained next day was a small charred peak at the centre of a circle of ash. Some fifteen years passed, and beside that blackened remnant a little shoot arose. It grew rapidly and today there is a fine, slender weeping willow throwing its young branches into the empty space. The parables of nature need no comment.

The gardener's house

From this part of the garden, one has a clear view of the long west front of the monastery, with the bell tower rising behind. Here the daily rhythm of Carmelite life unfolds, the various elements of work and prayer succeeding each other as predictably as the movements of a dance. This ordered routine, coloured by the liturgical cycle as the garden is coloured by the changing seasons of the year, is of the very substance of Carmel. The balanced pattern of its repetitions shapes the existence of the Carmelite, forming her to a simplicity and quietude that are the ground of habitual prayerfulness. Such, at any rate, is the ideal. Would that it always went as smoothly!

Each of the identical windows stretching along the upper storey of the house marks the cell of an individual sister. ('Cell' as in honeycomb, not as in prison!) This is her 'place apart', ensuring for her the measure of solitude necessary for contemplative living. Leading off the corridor where the cells are is the nuns' choir, or place of prayer, connected with the public chapel. Beneath the cells are the community room and the chapter room. These are the places where the group prays together, recreates together, reflects and discerns together. But in the cell each one is alone with God, available to the action of divine love slowly awakening her to truth.

Every Carmelite cell holds the story of ongoing conversion. The bare walls have witnessed hours of struggle and resistance, 'Lest, having Him, I must have naught beside.'[13] They have sheltered lonely times of near-despair in the face of personal weakness and inadequacy. They have firmly contained the restless spirit dreaming of less radical ways of answering the call that will not be silenced. The cell is home to the long stretches of 'ordinary time', in which a person learns what it means to live intent upon God, tending towards God in everything. And it guards graced moments of response to God's faithfulness and of tranquil union with the Beloved.

As the founding hermits of Carmel well knew, the cell nurtures the slow development of the life of prayer and self-offering that bears fruit in a growing sense of the divine presence at the centre of one's being. The mature Carmelite's knowledge of oneness with the life of God pervades, in the simplest possible way, her work, her prayer, her relations with others, her personal pursuits, all touched with a heightened awareness and attentiveness. It also makes increasingly refined demands. The light of Christ and his gospel reaches to deeper levels of life, revealing every self-serving, self-protecting attitude – to a degree that, while still painful, is ultimately welcomed as liberating. Indeed, the greatest freedom is to stand unafraid in one's own truth before the mystery of God's truth. Something in the human spirit hungers for this, persistently yearning for the full realisation of Christ's promise: 'When the Spirit of truth comes, he will lead you to the complete truth' (Jn 16:13). I think the essence of what Carmel means to me lies in this: that its whole spiritual teaching affirms and supports the pursuit of truth as the central quest of life. Carmel is nothing other than garden-space for this growth.

The garden enclosed

I have said above that the garden of Carmel has no frontiers, and yet I walk in a garden surrounded on all sides by a twenty-two foot wall! This formidable boundary effectively serves its purpose of ensuring seclusion for a sustained prayer-life in the midst of the city of London. It also symbolises the enclosed garden of the heart that has to be maintained in every walk of life if a spirit of prayer and interiority is to develop.

For the cloistered Carmelite, the lifetime practice of enclosure creates the ecosystem in which this comparatively rare vocation can best thrive. It has become all the more necessary in our age of increased speed and noise, resulting in a 'climate change' that is hostile to the contemplative spirit. Enclosure does not, however, constitute a conservation area for the preservation of an endangered species! There is sufficient bio-diversity within Carmel to suggest that the charism is robust enough to continue to re-express itself as the circumstances of its environment change. Indeed, one of the tasks engaging Carmelite nuns, as we move on into the twenty-first century, is the adaptation of centuries-old attitudes to reflect developments in the Church's self-understanding and the corresponding shift in our own understanding of our place within the Church. Carmel belongs to the Church and people of *today*.

A fruitful garden

If, as the culmination of a life of prayer, a person's surrender to the closeness of God's embrace makes her unafraid to claim her own truth, then she is finally free to make the full offering of herself, in union with Christ, for God's greater glory. Contained within this is the self-gift to all that is God's. It finds expression in concerned intercession, in genuine compassion and in willing service of others. In the final chapters of *The Interior Castle*, when Teresa is describing to her sisters what it means to have entered the soul's innermost dwelling where the King is in residence, the keyword is not 'bliss' but 'service'. The produce of Carmel's garden-land is for everyone, and its paths lead right to the heart of humanity.

Carmel has been my whole life for so long that it is difficult to step back sufficiently to identify the most significant aspects of what it means to me. I could have taken a completely different walk in the garden. I have simply followed a favourite route and shared the associations that came to me. Yet wherever else I might have lingered, I think the same key concepts would have emerged: life, growth and truth, together encompassing the compelling invitation to be made fruitful through love.

Notes

1. *The Collected Works of Saint John of the Cross*, Washington, DC: ICS Publications, 1991, pp. 110-111.
2. This work by Granada was, at the time Teresa read it, attributed to her friend St Peter of Alcántara: see *The Collected Works of St. Teresa of Avila*, vol. 2, Washington, DC: ICS Publications, 1980, p. 489, n. 7.
3. Hans Urs von Balthasar, *Prayer*, London: Geoffrey Chapman, 1961, p. 68.
4. *Story of a Soul: The Autobiography of Saint Thérèse of Lisieux*, Washington, DC: ICS Publications, 1996, p. 213.
5. In his famous drawing of Mount Carmel (see n. 1 above), John describes the path of ascent as 'nothing, nothing, nothing' – that is, the way of divesting ourselves of everything that is not God.
6. Thomas Merton, *Seeds of Contemplation*, London: The Catholic Book Club, 1950, p. 172.
7. Cf. 2A 5:6; 14:9; 16:10; 2DN 8:3-4; SC 26:17; LF 3:77.
8. *Story of a Soul, op. cit.*, p. 194.
9. Letter 310, in *Complete Works of Elizabeth of the Trinity*, vol. 2, Washington, DC: ICS Publications, 1995, p. 327.

10. Letter 124, in *ibid*., p. 53.

11. Letter 250, in *ibid*., p. 233.

12. *Story of a Soul*, *op. cit*., p. 194.

13. From 'The Hound of Heaven', in *The Works of Francis Thompson: Poems*, vol. 1, London: Burns, Oates & Washbourne, [1913], p. 107.

Some Forthcoming Titles from the Teresian Press

A Moment of Prayer – A Life of Prayer
 – Conrad De Meester, OCD

What Carmel Means to Me
 – Edited by James McCaffrey, OCD
 & Joanne Mosley

John of the Cross: Seasons of Prayer
 – Iain Matthew, OCD

How Do I Pray Today?
 – Edited by James McCaffrey, OCD
 & Joanne Mosley

Holiness for All:
Themes from St Thérèse of Lisieux
 – Aloysius Rego, OCD